On the Go

Written by Monica Hughes

trains

trams

We are going to look at trains, trams, trucks and buses.

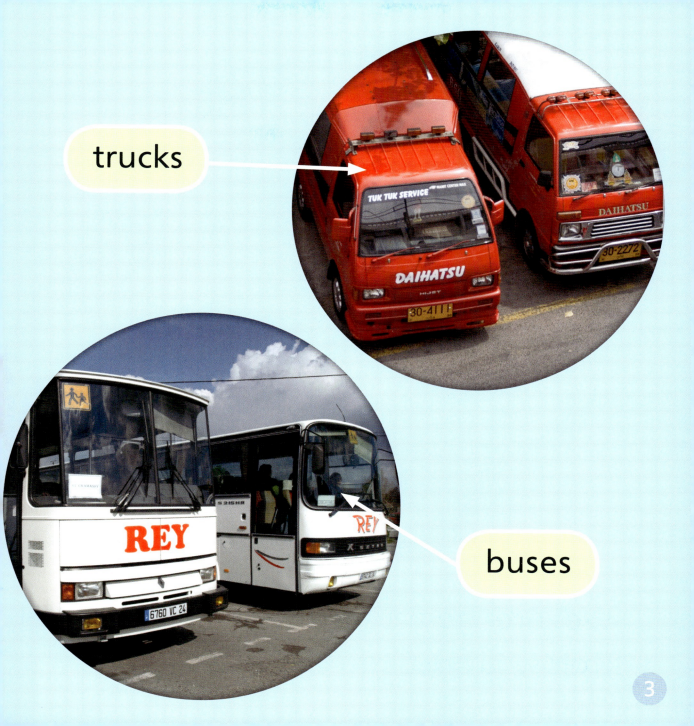

trucks

buses

3

Kids will get on this bus.

This coach will go on a long trip.

top deck

Look, this coach has a top deck.

film screen

We can see a film on a
screen in the coach.

rails

A tram runs on rails.

The rails are in the road.

Look at this long truck.

It is a road train.

The steel tank on this truck
is loaded with milk.

Sheep are loaded on trucks too.

Look at this high-speed train.
It is quick!

top deck

This is a high-speed train too.
It has a top deck.

This is not a high-speed train!